RENO'S WORLD

Presenting Autism and Related Disabilities To Youth

Reno Williams
Illustrations by Nikki Nacco

the Peppertree Press
Sarasota, Florida

The Adonis Autism Center of Southwest Florida
http://adonisautismflorida.com/

Copyright © Reno Williams, 2009

Graphic design by Rebecca Barbier. illustrations by Nikki Nacco

For information regarding permission,
call 941-922-2662 or contact us at our website:
www.peppertreepublishing.com or write to:
the Peppertree Press, LLC.
Attention: Publisher
1269 First Street, Suite 7
Sarasota, Florida 34236

ISBN: 978-1-936051-67-0

Library of Congress Number: 2009939527

Printed in the U.S.A.

Printed November 2009

For: my mom and dad

Introduction:

Right now, 1 out of 150 children are being diagnosed with an autism spectrum disorder. This means that there is a good chance that you will meet someone with autism either at the playground, school, church or out somewhere in the community. This book is to help grandparents, aunts, uncles, brothers, sisters, peers and educators understand a little more about children with autism and how to be a good friend to someone who has autism.

Acknowledgments:

I am very grateful for the continued support of my family, and for all the time, effort and inspiration that my mom and dad have given to me. I appreciate the countless hours waiting at doctor appointments, the endless IEP meetings to make sure that I am given the appropriate accommodations, supports and services at school and the hours my mom dedicates to researching new therapies and community activities. Thank you Mom and Dad for always being there for me and encouraging me in everything that I do- for always telling me that I have ONLY abilities and not focusing ever on my disabilities.

I want to thank my 5th grade teacher, Mrs. LaBelle, who pushed our class to enter the Thomas Edison Regional Science Fair. It was this project that inspired me to find out about myself and to teach others about autism. Without this experience, I don't know if I would be in the position I am in now of educating the community with my public speaking. Thank you so much Mrs. LaBelle!

I would like to say a very special thank you to Leigh Anna Nowak and the Center For Autism And Related Disabilities. Leigh Anna has helped me put all my hard work into brochures and power-points and helped me become the public speaker that I am today. She has accompanied me to all my speaking presentations, helped with the technical issues and has become a huge part of my life. Leigh Anna has helped me put all my dreams into reality. I could never thank Leigh Anna enough for everything she has done for me.

Without the help of the Adonis Autism Center of Southwest Florida, I would have never been able to have this book published. Thank you to everyone there for giving me this opportunity to be able to reach so many people. I will forever be grateful for this opportunity. Thank you so much!

Thanks to the wonderful people at The Peppertree Press. Julie Ann Howell and Terri Lynn Franco have been so wonderful and made the process of publishing my first book a smooth and easy one.

A very special thank you to my Aunt Nikki who dedicated her valuable time and hard work on creating the illustrations for my book.

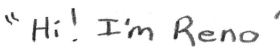

Hi, my name is Reno. I am ten years old and in the 5th grade. I look just like your typical kid. I have brown hair and green eyes. I guess for my age I am kind of short, and everybody always asks me, "When are you going to get some meat on you?" What? Get some meat on me? Are they crazy? Why would someone want me to have meat on me? All I could see is me with a huge steak hanging from my neck. I had no idea why someone would say that to me.

4

Well, so you can understand me a little better, I should mention to you that I have **Asperger's**. Asperger's?? Wow, what a big word. Asperger's is a neurobiological disorder (an illness of the nervous system) considered to be on the autism spectrum. Ugh....now we have even more words that are hard to understand. I am going to try to explain what Asperger's is so that you, your friends, your parents and even your brother or sister can understand.

OK, here goes....Sometimes I see things a little differently from you. For example, the comment that I mentioned earlier about when someone said to me, "When are you going to get some meat on you?" I literally (really) thought that they wanted me to walk around with meat on me.

Those sayings are called **idioms**. I only know that because my mom printed all of them out, and everyday we went over and over and over them. (She was trying to help me understand that they really didn't literally mean what they said). Some other examples of idioms are: the cow jumped over the moon and does the cat got your tongue?; just to name a couple.

Kids who have Asperger's think that what everyone says is true. We have a hard time understanding jokes, starting a conversation with another person, asking another kid to play with us, joining a group of kids in an activity, making eye contact with another person and understanding people's gestures (like when someone shrugs their shoulders or rolls their eyes).

I also do some things that other kids might not do, like when I get really excited, I jump up and down sometimes; my hands do this flapping thing like I'm about to fly off into space. Sometimes, I scream or make loud noises when I get really mad, sad or happy. (Sometimes, I can't even believe what I'm doing). But, it still happens; I have no control over it, and half the time I don't realize it until someone says... RENO?? But mostly it's my sister saying, "RENO!! STOP IT!!!"

6

Kids who have Asperger's also like to focus on certain subjects and that is all we can seem to think about or talk about, like maybe dinosaurs or past presidents. We learn everything about that particular subject and really become very knowledgeable about it.

Another thing that is very hard for me to do is change my routine; I have to know exactly what is coming next. I hate not knowing what is next, so a lot of kids who have Asperger's use picture schedules, charts or written schedules to follow for the day. This way we know exactly what is going to happen next.

Kids with Asperger's want to have friends too!

"Reno, You can use my hat if it is too bright!"

"Thank You!"

I just want everyone to know that kids with Asperger's look just like any other kid; we just think and act differently. We see the world in a different way and sometimes need a little help from the people around us.

8

Right now 1 kid out of 250 is being diagnosed with Asperger's (Asperger's Syndrome Coalition of US). The ratio of males to females is 4:1. That means more boys are being diagnosed than girls. To put it simply, there is a good chance that you will meet a kid who has autism or Asperger's sometime, maybe at school, church, or on the playground.

Just remember, they have feelings just like you!

How to be a good friend to Kids with Autism

Kids with autism look the same as you and me. They want and need friends just like you do. The only difference between them and you is they might need a little help in understanding how to play with you, how to start a conversation with you, how to start up a new game, or they may need help being included in a group. One important thing to remember is that autism is NOT contagious. This means that you cannot get autism from talking with, being with, or playing with someone who has autism.

The Golden Rule

Always treat another person the same way you would like to be treated, regardless if they do or do not have a disability.

More Alike than Different

HOW KIDS WITH AUTISM MAY BE THE SAME AS YOU

 They look the same as you (hair or eye color)

 They want and need friends

 They like to do the same things you do

 They love their family

 They like to play

HOW KIDS WITH AUTISM MAY BE DIFFERENT THAN YOU

 Their brain works in a different way

 They may need help...

    ...Understanding how to play with you

    ...How to start a conversation with you

    ...How to start up a new game

    ...How to be included in a group

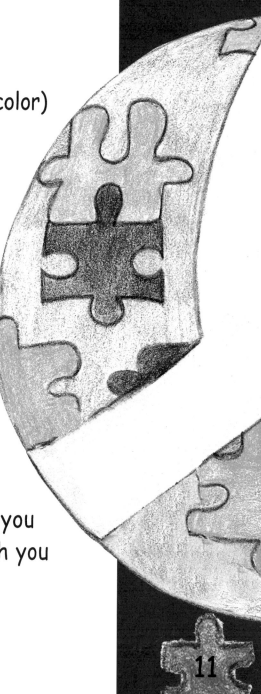

Understanding Kids with Autism

In the next few pages, the words in the yellow box represent some things that kids with autism might do that may be a little different. The words by the smiley face are some things that you can do to make everyone feel more comfortable.

Might flap their arms→	☺ Don't laugh, stare or call them names like retard or stupid
Might jump up and down→	☺ Try to ignore this behavior or maybe join in on it
Might not know how to ask you to play or how to think up a game to play with you→	☺ Take the first step and ask them to play with you and your friends

12

Might make sounds that sound silly, are annoying to others or are too loud →

☺ Don't be afraid, as long as they are not hurt, they are just expressing themselves

☺ Ask them to use an inside voice

☺ Get them involved in an activity they like to do

Try not to cover your ears or look scared, and don't laugh or make fun of their noises.

Might stay on a certain subject that they like or know a lot about →

☺ Try asking them questions about the subject they like, you'll be amazed how much you can learn from a friend who has autism.

☺ Set a time limit, then ask them to talk about a subject you are interested in

☺ Find an activity you are both interested in

13

Might find it hard to go from one activity to another without any warning of the new activity ➜

☺ Try to set time limits and explain what the next activity is

☺ "in 10 minutes we are going to do this_____"

Their brain just works in a different way than yours and they may need a little more help in several areas of social communication, understanding language, play and interacting with others. Help be a good friend by asking another kid to join in and play, be respectful, kind and thoughtful of other's feelings.

Might yell, swear or scream and become very upset for what seems like no reason ➜

☺ Try to stay calm

☺ Don't yell or scream back

☺ Find an adult or teacher to help with the situation

Might get upset easily by bright lights, sounds, smells, tastes or touches →	☺ Play inside if the sun is too bright, or suggest sunglasses ☺ Move away from bothersome smells, don't wear perfume or body-spray if it will bother your friend ☺ Change activities if it is upsetting your friend

Sometimes you may need to go away from the smell with your friend until that smell is gone. You may have to change an activity if they don't like the feel of something like sand or playdough. Maybe you can draw or play a board game. Sometimes they may spit out certain foods when they first feel it in their mouth, try telling them to put it in a napkin and ask the person who prepared the food to try something different.

15

You can be a good friend by:

- 😊 Asking another kid to join in and play
- 😊 Being respectful, kind and thoughtful of others feelings
- 😊 Never laughing at or calling someone names
- 😊 Never pushing, or hitting another person
- 😊 Never making fun of another person
- 😊 Never joining in with a bully
- 😊 Telling an adult if someone is being mean to another person
- 😊 Never yelling at someone (use your inside voice)
- 😊 Sitting next to your new friend in class or the lunchroom
- 😊 Not ignoring anyone

Being cool is:
being responsible, respectful, and reliable, making good choices, and being a good friend!

What is Autism (aw-tiz-um)?

    Autism is a severe life-long developmental disorder that affects the way a child sees and interacts with the world around him or her.

    According to the Centers for Disease Control and Prevention's ADDME autism report (February 2007), autism has risen to 1 out of 150 American children and almost 1 in 94 boys. This means there is a good chance that you will meet someone on the autism spectrum. Kids who have autism share similar symptoms, but each child with autism acts very differently.

Some common signs of autism in children are:

- lack of or delay in spoken language (talking, speaking)
- repetitive (repeated) use of language and or motor mannerisms (e.g. – hand flapping, twirling objects)
- little or no eye contact
- lack of interest in peer relationships (making friends)
- lack of spontaneous (without previous thought or planning) make-believe play
- persistent fixation on part of objects (constant, overly strong attachment to a person, idea or thing)

Some behavioral symptoms might be:

- hyperactivity (not being able to sit still)
- short attention span (not be able to pay attention for a long period of time)
- impulsivity (acting on impulse – a sudden desire to do something)
- aggressiveness (fierce or threatening behavior)
- self-injurious behavior (hurting themselves)
- temper tantrums

- trouble sleeping
- sensitivity to light or sounds (easily bothered by)
- irritable (cross and grumpy)
- agitated (nervous or worried)

(Information taken from the Autism Society of America and Center for Autism and Related Disabilities)

Trying to explain autism and autism relate disabilities is sometimes very hard. I will try t explain it to you the way I learned about it.

The term pervasive developmental disability (the act o developing) or PDD refers to a group of conditions tha involve delays in development of many different basi skills like the ability to socialize with others, communi cate and use imagination.

The 5 pervasive developmental disorders are al considered to be on the autism spectrum.

Think of the spectrum as a line.

Autism	Childhood Disintegrative Disorder	Rett's Syndrome	PDD-NOS Pervasive Developmental Disorder Not Otherwise Specified	Asperger's Syndrome

18

AUTISM (aw-tiz-um) - Kids with autism have problems with social interaction, pretend play and communication. Sometimes they cannot speak with words. They also have a limited range of activities and interests. Autism can occur with or without mental retardation (to have a diagnosis of mental retardation the person has to have both a significantly low IQ and problems in everyday functioning) or other health problems. Autism is usually recognized during the first three years of a child's life.

CHILDHOOD DISINTEGRATIVE DISORDER - This is a very rare disorder. Kids start developing normally; then between the ages of 2-10 years they start to lose many of their social and language skills that they have already learned. They also may not be able to control their bowel and bladder (How they go to the bathroom).

RETT'S SYNDROME - This is also a rare disorder. Children have the symptoms associated with a PDD but also have problems with physical development. They lose skills like walking and using their hands. This condition is linked to a defect on the X chromosome, so it almost always affects girls. The X chromosome is one of two sex chromosomes in humans; the other is the Y chromosome. A chromosome is formed from a single DNA molecule that contains many genes.

PERVASIVE DEVELOPMENTAL DISORDER NOT OTHERWISE SPECIFIED (PDD-NOS) - Kids in this category have many problems with communication, play and interacting appropriately with others but are too social to be considered autistic.

ASPERGER'S SYNDROME - Like kids with autism, children with Asperger's have difficulty with social interaction and communication, poor eye contact and understanding gestures and facial expressions. They may be interested only in certain subjects, might display certain talents, may sometimes have strange rituals or use repetitive speech and may interpret literal meanings to idioms which are sayings or expressions like "the cow jumped over the moon." However, children with Asperger's have average or above average intelligence and develop normally in the areas of language and cognition, the mental processing related to thinking and learning.

CPSIA information can be obtained
at www.ICGtesting.com
Printed in the USA
LVIC072150060213

318992LV00005B